10 Must-Do, Tried and True
Secrets In Getting Syndicated

SYNDICATION *SECRETS*

What No One Will Tell You!

Jodie Lynn

**Internationally Syndicated
Parent/Family Columnist
of *Parent to Parent*™ and
Best-Selling Author of
*Mommy CEO, revised edition***

Syndication Secrets - What No One Will Tell You!

By Jodie Lynn

Book Cover Design by Jamie Jones, Jackson Marketing & Printing Services, LLC

Library of Congress Catalog Number:
ISBN 978-1-933476-60-5
ISBN 1-933476-60-5

Stacey Kannenberg Unlimited
N6854 Cedar Valley Road
Fredonia, WI 53021

Imprint of Cedar Valley Publishing

Printed in the United States

Dedication

This book is dedicated to every person who wants to move closer to their goal of becoming a syndicated columnist. For those who tried and tried but could not make that one final step and ended up changing plans or giving up on their dream, here's hoping that my words and secrets can ignite that fire you once had in the pit of your soul - it can happen!

Find one or two people who can be your support system. If it had not been for a 66-year-old grandmother who was also a columnist, I would have tossed in the towel. Thanks, Dottie, you made a world of difference!

Thanks also goes to my good friend Stacey Kannenberg. Thanks so much for your continued support and inspiration in moving me forward in my career. Your friendship will always be treasured!

Last, but not least, to my editor, Curtis Peck. No matter what kind of a mood I am in, you always bring a smile to my heart.

Contents

Chapter One

Chapter Two

Chapter Three

Chapter Four

Chapter Five

Chapter Six

Chapter Seven

Chapter Eight

<u>Chapter Nine</u>

<u>Chapter Ten</u>

Preface

So, you want to get a column into the syndication world? Then get ready to read this book from cover to cover and to work harder than you ever have before. Get started on securing your place in the syndication world today.

Begin by reviewing these important questions:

* Do you really have what it takes to go head-to-head with those in the big leagues?

* Can you "show and tell" them how your idea is different from the other 20 proposals they received just that morning?

* Can you take the rejection letters and the negative responses and offer a professional rebuttal?

*   If all else fails, can you make it by self-syndicating?

If you have answered "No!" to any (or all) of these questions:

IT DOES NOT MATTER. This book will show you how to supercharge your brain and plug into your talents with my sometimes quirky but always effective secrets. I am going to share tried and true tips that no one else will give you. With hard work and constant persistence, they have worked for me and I believe they will work for you.

Just remember: Through it all, believe in yourself, your ideas and your goals.

Move forward with inspiration, determination and gusto!

Introduction

Hi, my name is Jodie Lynn. Like you, I wanted to write a column, get it into newspapers, and then accomplish the ultimate objective: Get it syndicated.

I decided to take syndication in baby steps and began with trying to get a column published by a local newspaper. When my family and friends laughed (which got me a bit annoyed), this only made me more determined.

In the beginning, I wrote a column called "Good Parents Made Better," which was based on a series of parenting classes that I taught. This was successful in small but significant ways, so I thought, "OK, why not try for newspapers?"

Long story made short, I changed the format in 1995 for better newspaper appeal and gave my column a new name - one suggested by a newspaper editor. My column was published for the first time in 1996 under the new name **Parent to Parent™**.

That's right, my column made it into newspapers with a new name and a new format. I have been writing the column for nearly 11 years. I have been syndicated for seven of those years, but nothing has been easy. In saying this, I want you to realize that, from talking to other columnists, I have found out that sometimes it takes what seems to be a lifetime to accomplish the task of just getting into one paper.

Some syndication veterans told me that they have been writing a column for 15 or so years, and me being able to get my column syndicated in only two years, well, that is a huge success story. It is one that is just as inspiring today as it was yesterday because the column continues to grow.

With this in mind, I am going to share my insights and my secrets with you. I'll also tell you some of the pitfalls. Although it didn't take much time to syndicate the column once I started writing it, it did take several years to actually get it into a newspaper on a weekly basis.

There are lots of people who want to write a column or a book or who aspire to follow through on many other writing opportunities. I will tell you right now: It is hard work, and there are far more failures than there are success stories.

To me, syndication is the ultimate satisfaction; it tells you that you have made it, and that all of your hard work has paid off. There have been very few books written on the "how to" of this amazingly difficult task, and few are willing to share the real secrets of syndication.

Here is what I recommend to you if you want to become a syndicated columnist: Read a bit of this book every day, practice what I am going to share with you, add your own personality to the guidelines, be patient, ask a lot of questions and NEVER GIVE UP. I will show you how to turn negative responses into positive, constructive ideas that will make you more focused and enable you to become successful. I did it, and so can you!

Keep in mind that I am sharing my experiences from the perspective of being syndicated in a print newspaper and not a magazine, an online publication or a radio show.

Whichever way you are thinking about going, these syndication rules will be able to help. Here are some things that worked for me and, while there are very few guarantees in life, this book will help get you started on the right track in just about any syndication endeavor.

I have written a couple of books, the one before this being "Mommy-CEO" (2001, revised edition), and I have contributed to a couple of others. One in 2002 (which was on "The Oprah Winfrey Show" and even sponsored in part by her media company, Oxygen Media) titled "The Entrepreneurial Parent," and another, in 2003, "Why Aren't You Your Own Boss?" I was on NBC for three months for parenting segments. I gave the TV segments up to sign a contract with Oprah's Oxygen.com.

I currently write for several Web sites, provide two-minute parenting tips for radio shows, and am working on yet another book, **Mom CEO (Chief Everything Officer)™ - Having, Doing, and Surviving It All!** plus a few other endeavors, including being the spokesperson for Stacey Kannenberg Unlimited, an Imprint of Cedar Valley Publishing and BabyUniverse.com. (See ParentToParent.com for more details.) This is one of the rewards of having a syndicated column: Your name gets around and opportunities pop up. Who knows - it could happen to you!

CHAPTER ONE

Prepare for a Bumpy Ride

Rule Number 1:
Believe in what you have to say.

Then, be prepared for a long and bumpy ride. I want to let you know right away that it is not easy to get syndicated, and literally thousands are turned down.

Prepare yourself for rejection. It may even happen over and over. You can compare the feat of achieving syndication to that of a high school athlete going on to play for a professional team. Something like one out of every 50,000 make it. Not only is that incredibly hard to swallow, but most syndicated columnists have other jobs just to make ends meet because the syndicate takes at least 40-60 percent from the sales of their column. It's hard to make big bucks until you get popular enough to get numerous speaking engagements and/or offers for lucrative book or endorsement contracts.

You may also be approached with a contract to supply a column or article for a Web site, obtain a deal for a TV segment/radio show or encounter other column-related moneymaking opportunities. Even if these things do happen, it may take years to make really good money.

Submitting Your Column:

Believe in your idea.

If you still want to write a column after what I have just told you, then I hope your reason for doing so is one of these:

1. You are hoping to fill a niche and don't care about the initial moneymaking process.

2. You want to help improve society (and do not care about the money).

3. You love competition and are set on winning this one for all of the right reasons. If this is the case, half of the battle is won.

Jodie's Secret:

Begin with a single newspaper.

I started out trying to get my column idea into a newspaper

simply because in doing research looking for a column that might feature an idea similar to mine, I found very few in the city where we lived. Getting a column picked up by a newspaper is a major undertaking. You have to be sold on your column idea and then sell the newspaper editor on the idea.

Here's how my column concept came about:

I taught parenting classes, which I kind of fell into by accident. I was always taking parenting classes and adding my two cents about life, kids and being a mom. I thought I was a good parent, but I wanted to be better, hence the title of my original column, "Good Parents Made Better."

One day, the facilitator at one of the parenting classes I was taking could not make it to class. She called and asked if I would fill in for her. It turned out that she was not able to return to class at all, and I ended up becoming a permanent "fill-in." I really began to get into leading the class. I thought it was fun. I had an opportunity to learn from the other parents, who I have always said seemed to know more about parenting challenges than the authors of most of the books we were using. In fact, this was the pitch I used to the newspapers for my column idea. I voiced the opinion that no one ever let the parents have a say in any of the parenting columns and articles. The "experts" who wrote them just told parents what to do but never seemed to listen.

Often, the so-called experts did not even have children, and if they did, a nanny was raising them. The newspaper editors did not seem to buy my philosophy at all. At the time I approached them several years ago, not much was known about the power of moms and how they influence the success of columns. Today, "mom power" has become quite a force in the business world.

Moms are the big spenders and make most of the buying decisions in the household. Businesses have finally caught on to this and have changed many aspects of their marketing appeal to capitalize on this newfound respect for moms. Companies now realize that moms who work from the home, outside the home or who are stay-at-home moms raising their kids have too significant an economic say to be so ignored any longer. In fact, one of the web sites I write for, ClubMom.com, saw a huge opportunity in providing convenient online shopping for moms. In addition, to offering hundreds of products that moms usually buy everyday, they also offer a wealth of knowledge on literally hundreds of topics. This revelation has changed the way many an editor perceives the success of column content and its appeal to readers.

My pitch to treat moms (and dads) as the real experts in child-rearing was ahead of its time 10 years ago and may be the reason many originally scoffed at the idea. But I was the one teaching parenting classes and knew the value of input from parents, so I stuck with it.

Always believe in yourself, no matter what others may say.

CHAPTER TWO

Know Your Competition

Rule Number 2:
Check various directories.

Know your competition. Find out if others already have implemented your column idea. One good source is The Editor and Publisher Annual Directory of Syndication, available annually. It can be found in bookstores and on EditorandPublisher.com. This Web site also has a lot of other timely information that may help you in your research.

Submitting Your Column:

Compare your idea to others.

Do a search on the Internet and see who is writing what

and read some of their columns. This is something I could not do back in 1994. The Internet was not prominent then, so I looked for information in books at the library and in as many newspapers as I could get my hands on.

Read everything you can about anyone who might be writing along the same lines as what you want to do. Compare what they are doing and see if your idea is different. But if it is not vastly different, do not let that stop you.

Your idea about a column could be unique in presentation or even in format. For example (keep in mind that this example is related to building a successful and creative business), Martha Stewart came up with her own magazine even though similar publications such as Good Housekeeping, Southern Living, Midwest Living and tons of others were already available.

Stewart made hers different by naming the magazine after herself and focusing on her trademark talents. She personalized the articles just enough to set the whole magazine apart and make the readers feel as if the advice of one well-known woman - not a nameless writing staff - was coming directly to them.

The public loved the one-woman show. I am sure there were many people who thought that they had creative ideas and suggestions for Stewart, but she knew the direction she wanted for the magazine and for her show and stuck with her own winning insight - and it proved to be a huge success.

Here's an example of the comparison idea: If I wanted to write about cars, I would look for columnists in that category. I would cut out or print out from magazines, newspapers or online material some columns I could relate to. I would look for what was missing - things that would allow me to write a successful column without changing my ideas or copying another's writing style.

I will never forget one day when I was preparing to do a speaking engagement. I began to get nervous as I talked with other columnists and writers about writing styles. They were discussing how during most "question and answer" sessions, people would want to know about your writing style. I had no idea what they were talking about. I ran to a bookstore and carried an armful of books to a table to see which ones I might need to buy to learn more about writing style.

An older, well-known columnist happened to be in the bookstore at that time. She asked me what I was doing and I told her. She laughed so hard, she had to sit down. "Jodie, those books are not going to contain any kind of a revelation into your personal writing style, nor or they going to make anything 'better;' they will only confuse you. Your writing style is what it is: natural, creative, personal, caring and other good things that are missing in so many others. Just leave well enough alone."

Since she had been a successful columnist and author for more than 20 years, I took her advice and put all of the books back (to the chagrin of the sales clerk) and went on my merry little way, knowing that her words of wisdom were beyond what any book could ever teach me.

Jodie's Secret:

Fill a niche in today's society.

Can you fill a niche? While you are researching who writes about the topic you are interested in, make a list of comparisons to see if your column would really fill a niche.

I did not know anything about any type of directories where columns of any kind could be checked. I did not even know that there was a National Society of Newspaper Columnists until the past couple of years! No one ever told me anything, especially since I came from a teaching background as opposed to one in journalism. But after reviewing tons of papers, I knew I had not seen anything yet that even came close to providing the information - filling the niche - that my column did.

When I wanted to begin my question-and-answer column on parenting, I could not find a single columnist doing the same thing except perhaps Ann Landers and Dear Abby. They did not write much on parenting topics back then, however, and their columns did not appeal to me because I needed more specific family topics covered - things that I and a zillion other sleep-deprived parents were going through and couldn't find in a newspaper. I made up a list of parenting dilemmas that would drive me crazy every day - simple but exhausting stuff, such as handling colic, feeding a new baby, dealing with more than one child, making your partner happy and getting more than one leg at a time shaved. (This was in the first 10 minutes of the first day of my journaling!)

Each day the list grew longer, and I tried to read books but could find none that did cover this "everyday," pull-your-hair-out stuff without a three-chapter rendition of mumbo-jumbo, psychological and academic jargon. I just wanted quick tips that were from real people! In everything I looked over, those simple, down-to-earth answers were not to be found.

I looked around to see if I could find someone whom I might be able to use as a role model, and who might inspire me to be similar in likes and dislikes. As much as I wanted to have a role model, I could not find one. I was so sick of "experts," I wanted to upchuck.

I never wanted to be an expert, and the first time I heard myself being labeled as one, I thought I might pass out! I wanted to buck the system - the one thing I was best known for - and to create a column that would benefit readers every day in a quick and easy way by offering them a platform to network.

I saw this best being done by printing their own tried-and-true tips in the column and adding their names, cities and states. This would be different from anything I had seen and was giving credit where credit was due.

Experts never offered a "pat on the back" to parents, and would go on and on about a cause and effect, ending up not only losing the meaning of what the column or article was supposed to be about in the first place, but also failing to get around to answering the original question!

In fact, they left readers wondering about other things we

had not even thought about before. While this can be good in many ways, as parents, we need to get a quick answer to a dilemma without feeling as if we were going to damage our children for the rest of their lives for not letting them have the red balloon instead of the blue one, or whatever.

The one thing I kept coming back to was that I felt as if I had a new design for specific goals and strived for that uniqueness. This is what it is all about: filling a niche.

Keep in mind that many columns are quite short and are getting shorter. Understanding this is crucial to your success. Why? It is simple: Since columns are getting briefer because of the constant budget and space challenges today's newspapers face, a column often will omit key information, especially if it is written by an author who does not have the same life experiences as you do.

Look to see if the columns are not saying enough about a topic that you deem important. Maybe this can become a springboard for you. Scrutinize the columns and see what's missing and try to make your column include as much of those missing components as possible.

But even if you cannot come up with something distinctive, do not change your idea until the change is one you are wholeheartedly behind.

Think about it: You have come up with a brainchild and feel strongly about it. Even if you have never had any experience in writing a column before, listen to your heart and follow your passion.

That is why people such as Martha Stewart, Oprah Winfrey and Dr. Phil have been so immensely successful - they followed their own heart, spirit and dream.

These are not the only people that I hold dear to my heart, but the three of them are individuals from whom we can all learn something from by simply watching, learning and evaluating our own lives.

Each of them has made mistakes, just like everyone does. This keeps them human and maintains an element that real people such as you and I can connect with on a personal basis.

Keeping things down to earth and staying real is a key factor in why some people succeed while others do not.

Always be true to your own inner spirit!

CHAPTER THREE

Confirm Your Idea

Rule Number 3:
Get opinions.

Confirm your column idea. You think you have a strong creative foundation for a column, but try to imagine what total strangers would think of it. Go ask.

Submitting Your Column:

Get public feedback.

Filling a void in the field of your expertise is important. The syndicates and/or editorial staff are looking for a column that can be profitable and bring in new readership. While your family and friends may support you, they are not the ones you need to impress.

Make up and conduct your own poll. Public feedback is essential in helping you determine how your column will be received by readers. The most crucial step in this part of your plan is asking strangers their opinions. Their answers provide you with insightful information that is not biased and, interestingly, prepares you for more rejections from the editorial staff at the newspaper or at the syndicates. Believe me, there will be a few hundred rejections. Well, maybe not hundreds, but it will sure feel like it.

As I stood just outside the path of the crowded escalator in one of the largest malls in America during one of the busiest times of the year, I had to get creative to get people to stop and talk with me.

One day, I dressed up like a witch to see how many would take the time to answer my questions. The next time, I came as Superwoman; that time, I got more than 50 responses.

Another weekend, I went into the playground at a Burger King, and was barely able to hear responses. Nevertheless, moms were very willing to chat.

Yet another time that flashes before my eyes is the time I waited inside the ladies room of a nice restaurant and talked to women as they washed their hands. One asked if I would go to the stall next to the one she had to go back into, so I did. We talked and laughed at what others might be thinking as we carried on a six-minute conversation.

What was all of this about? Back in 1995, I had pitched a parenting column to a newspaper and they had turned me down because the editorial staff thought no one would be interested. Therefore, I set out to prove them wrong.

I asked every parent and grandparent I could find what they thought of the idea. My idea was to have a small column with "tried and true tips" from other parents/grandparents on family challenges. It would cover one "head-exploding" challenge at a time for quick answers. Every person I interviewed was very much in favor of it - except my own friends and family.

They laughed and said no one would ever buy a newspaper column from someone who had never written before. Boy, were they wrong.

When I presented a newspaper's editorial staff with the findings of my survey, they looked and sounded shocked. Then they asked me to come in and sign a contract for a 90-day trial period. The column started in February 1996, and was so popular the contract was redone in 30 days.

One year later, my editor asked for an update on my plans for the column. I said that since parents from all over the United States were writing to me, maybe we could get it syndicated. Again, everyone scoffed.

Well, to make a long story short, I got pretty creative on that one, too. One year later, a syndicate wanted to syndicate the column! Today, a potential 19 million readers in the United States and Canada read it!

Jodie's Secret:

Keep good records.

Ask everyone you know about your idea, and ask if they would read a column like the one you are describing, whether it was in the newspaper, online or in a magazine. Keep accurate records of all responses and do not forget to date all of your material. In my case, I failed to get one "no."

Everyone I asked said they would be happy to read a brief column in a newspaper on parenting (online columns were pretty scarce at that time). Men and women alike said that they would welcome a parenting column for quick tips, especially if others going through a similar situation were sharing their experiences. What could be better?

This was exactly how I felt, as did the other moms and dads - teachers, too - whom I had discussed it with. Teachers who also were parents often said they could implement parenting and family guidelines right into the classroom.

Everyone was impressed with the fact that my main goal was to treat everyday folks as the heart and soul of the column, highlighting them in an unreached area - as being the real experts. Moms and dads were thrilled that someone was willing to listen to the tried and true remedies that had helped them work through a difficult time with their kids. It was an amazing opportunity to build a reputable platform for parents to network together on various parenting issues and not feel all alone or guilty at the choices that they made.

That was the amazing joy, the lost whisper of the voices of other parents sharing their mistakes as well as good experiences with others in order to regain their sanity and help others rely on their own judgment on the common ground of this crazy thing called parenting.

Armed with this poll and comment sheet, I was surer then than I had ever been that my plan for a parenting/ family column would fill a niche. If all of these strangers had placed their faith in me, I had to be sure to give it everything I could.

Find your inner spirit and let it ignite your dreams!

CHAPTER FOUR

Overcoming Objections

Rule Number 4:

Be prepared.

Prepare early for objections - an editorial staff will have plenty. Have your answers ready and be well prepared with strong rebuttals.

Ask yourself the following "on the spot questions" that the editorial staff or syndicate may ask you. Although I have not touched upon all of the questions, I will. Take a look at these and see how you can best overcome any objections.

(NOTE: Please take advantage of the ample space I have tried to leave you between certain areas to make notes right in the book. Write in pencil so your notes can be easily changed if needed.)

The 10 Most Common Objections You Will Face When Presenting Your Column to Editors, and How To Overcome Those Objections

Objection One:

HOW IS YOUR COLUMN DIFFERENT?

Show and tell them how your column is different by providing comparisons using other similar columns and pointing out what those columns are missing. Show how your column supplies the needed information - fills the niche. Studying other columns similar to yours will take some time and effort on your part, but it will pay off.

(Notes)

Objection Two:

WHY DO YOU THINK IT WILL SELL?

Focus on pointing out what other columns have not covered in the area you want to write. Make specific comparisons so the editors will know exactly what you are talking about. Contrast how a similar columnist handled a topic and how you wrote about it. Use a highlighter to highlight the differences, and go the extra mile by rating the differences on a scale of 1 to 5, with 5 being the biggest difference. Emphasize how your column will attract readers by giving them information that other columns fail to provide.

(notes)

Objection Three:

WHY SHOULD THE SYNDICATE CARRY YOUR COLUMN?

They should carry it:

- To make more money
- To be diverse
- To offer communities better connections with everyday life.
- To be the first to implement a new idea. Let them know that the people you have talked to - potential readers -

say your column meets a need they have, and tell them how you accomplish that.

(notes)

Objection Four:

WHAT NICHE WILL YOUR COLUMN FILL?

Show them sample columns that demonstrate how your writings fill a niche. Provide similar columns written by others and show how there is a certain area those columns miss and that your column will cover. This is similar to Objection 2, but in a second example, print the words, "My column fills a niche because" (and state the reason). Be prepared to discuss your rating system and why the ones you have marked as a 5 are key differences.

(notes)

Objection Five:

HOW WOULD THE SYNDICATE PITCH YOUR COLUMN TO NEWSPAPERS?

Think about an innovative way for them to pitch your column to the newspapers. You can even call newspaper editors yourself and ask them how they would pitch it to the readers. If you call in the mornings in the early part of the week, you will usually get through. Deadlines for the sections you are interested in often are in the middle to the latter part of the week. Remember this time element, as it is very critical to your contact attempt.

(notes)

Objection Six:

ARE YOU WILLING TO CHANGE THE COLUMN A LITTLE?

They may ask you to change it slightly. If you can be flexible and go with their suggestions without giving up the original concept, do it - but get everything in writing. Oral agreements will not hold up in court should some issue come up down the road. Get all revisions and agreements in writing. Should they send you a copy and ask you to sign it, be sure to ask for a signed copy by them for your own records.

(notes)

Objection Seven:

HOW LONG HAVE YOU BEEN WRITING?

If you have been writing a column since middle school for the school newspaper and on from there, this certainly counts. Tell them about any and all writing experience you have had. It will demonstrate your writing experience, show that you have been published and will illustrate your determination.

(notes)

Objection Eight:

WHAT MAKES YOUR COLUMN COMPELLING?

Again, tell how your column has appealed to others who have read it and tell them who the readers were: strangers, family, friends, teachers, other columnists, etc. Offer their comments, and tell how you have worked on your idea for several months or perhaps even years. Explain that you have monitored other columnists for a while and have seen none who meets the need that you do.

(notes)

Objection Nine:

ARE YOU WILLING TO HAND OVER THE COPYRIGHT FOR TWO WEEKS?

If you are signing a contract with a syndicate, make sure you have a lawyer go over it with a fine-tooth comb because the copyright laws are always changing.

For example, in my contract with a syndicate, I asked for the copyright of my column, **Parent to Parent™**, to revert to me in three days after a column was published. They insisted on making it seven days. This was fine with me. What this means is that they can publish the column in any form anywhere for seven days. After that period, the ownership and copyright come back to me, and I can do with it whatever I want - sell it to other businesses, magazines, parenting publications, Internet Web sites, etc. Again, get everything in writing with signatures from all parties involved.

(notes)

Objection Ten:

ARE YOU WILLING TO SIGN A SIX-MONTH CONTRACT?

The syndicate may ask for as little as a six-month contract or one as long as until either party - the syndicate or you - gives a 30-day written notice to end it. This is why I say you should offer a free trial for 60 to 90 days at no expense to them. They will have little to lose and will not owe you a cent. I will elaborate on this later in Chapter 9.

(notes)

Submitting Your Column:

Role-play.

Learn the answers to the above questions and feel good about them. In today's fast-paced society, when you get an interview, it will go quickly so it's important to be at your best for it. Role-play with someone who can offer constructive criticism.

Go over questions such as: What can you bring to the table that is different? How can your column find a niche in today's society? Why do you think it will be successful? What research have you done on it? Why would people be interested in it? Are you willing to be flexible with the format?

A column has to be formatted for use in a newspaper or magazine as well as online. The Internet has made many of the already tough rules even tougher. For example, a column for a newspaper will often times be designed for a specific format set by the editor or syndicate. They will usually have their own suggestions on how best it will fit into their paper for space and clarity.

Magazines and online publications have their own rules and guidelines, as well. Despite what others may tell you, you will have to learn as you go and either accept or reject their suggestions.

In today's world, Google owns the Internet. In fact, Google has just come up with an idea that in order for a site to be rated higher when "Googled," an article on that site needs to be different. In other words, I send out articles to several sites each month. If the articles are all the same, which I do often for convenience, then that column or article may not rank as well as if I send out several different articles to various sites. That is a new rule implemented in mid-2005 by Google.

However, if the site is a mega-player, such as eDiets.com, then the articles pretty much stay in the high ranks. I started writing for eDiets.com in 2004 in the Healthy Kids section. The site now has 10 million subscribers and is growing at a phenomenal rate.

Jodie's Secret:

Reaffirm your goals.

I talked to as many people as I could about my column. We had already lived in several cities and states, making it possible for me to get opinions from a variety of parents, teachers and even doctors. Every time I asked my questions, I was reaffirmed with the same answers: They wanted (and needed) quick tips and loved the idea of letting parents, teachers, etc., contribute.

Parents and teachers are busy people. While newspapers are cutting down on word count, my specific audience does not seem to mind. Ideally, you will want to register a domain in the same name of your column and create your own Web site.

By doing so, you are ensuring that your name and the name of your column is validated. When you go the extra steps by registering a domain with the name of your column, you are offering people and businesses a place to go to check it out. You are also displaying a serious, yet professional image detailing your legal rights to your columns and whatever else you might embark upon utilizing the name - such as on books or other merchandise. Always place the copyright symbol on your site and a trademark symbol on any catchy words or phrases that you feel might be interesting to the public.

When someone begins to write a column, most do not think this far in advance. For example, in the beginning, I had not thought of writing a book or using the inspiring title on merchandise. However, as soon as I published my first book, I knew the title was a winner simply based on feedback from moms. I immediately began to offer cups and T-shirts right out of my home with the **Mommy CEO™** logo as well as several other "CEO" logos and acronyms.

Recently, I was in an out-of-court battle with AOL/Time Warner. One of its vice presidents had "come up" with an idea that, suspiciously, had already been thought of in 1996 by me.

I wrote to the company and called its office after reading about the idea in the newspaper and online. The company called me back. I saved a recording of the message and called my attorney. From there, we went back and forth with the company's attorney and executive board members. After a yearlong battle, I won.

My determination to retain what was rightfully mine was

exhausting. I had to come up with all kinds of proof that I indeed coined the term **Mommy CEO™**, **Mom CEO™** and the various acronyms to go along with them. (If you are interested in learning more, see www.ParentToParent.com for details.)

My point is, do not allow the bigwigs to push you around when you know you are right. And always keep good records, complete with dates. In fact, as soon as you put an idea into action on the Web, add the trademark symbol. If and when a situation similar to mine arises, or whatever the situation may entail, if you have that trademark symbol up on the Internet, it is likely to prevail in most cases.

For example, if you have a catchy phrase or title such as **Mom CEO (Chief Everything Officer)™** and your attorney and you have done the research to be sure no one else has trademarked, used it online, in books or on merchandise, before you did, you are likely to prevail in any legal situation.

A word to the wise: Name your column, get a domain name immediately and get the trademark symbol up as soon as possible. Even if you are not prepared to go "live" with your site, at least buy and register the domain.

If the domain name is already taken, you can either wait for it to become available or change the name of your column. For example, I had to wait two years before the **Parent to Parent™** name became available.

You are a winner - act like one!

CHAPTER FIVE

Be Persistent

Rule Number 5:
Get the right contact information.

Call for the right contact information to send in your column. If the syndicate or the newspaper has the editorial-submission guidelines listed on its Web site, follow them. Most everyone's guidelines will ask for a query letter. Either way, a phone call cannot hurt and might even help.

Submitting Your Column:

Get your foot inside the door.

It is your responsibility to find out whom to send the column to so that it gets into the right hands. Getting your foot in the door of a newspaper or a syndicate can be a daunting task. I learned very quickly that newspaper editors and syndicates get about a million "ideas" sent to them for a column on a monthly basis. Keep a 5-by-7 index card on every action you take on every contact you have with the editor, assistant to the editor, voice mail or e-mail. Date the information - always date everything - and include the year, not just the month and date.

Jodie's Secret:

Never give up.

Call the right department. I searched the paper to see which area my column would most likely fit. I called the newspaper and asked for the name of the editor who might take a look at new ideas for columns. There are tons of different departments, and the newspaper's receptionist will float you from one to the other if you do not have the right one.

Tell the receptionist a little about what it is you want. By the end of the call, make sure you know which section of the paper and/or person will be the right one for your idea.

Tips to remember when calling for name and contact information:

1. Call the receptionist first.

2. Tell the receptionist who you are and what information you need.

3. Be polite to everyone you talk with. The person you may be asking information about could possibly be covering for the receptionist who has just left for lunch. No kidding - this has happened several times to me.

Sample Phone Script:

Editor: "Features department."

Jodie: "Hello, my name is Jodie Lynn. Is this the editor of the features department?"

Editor: "Yes, how can I help you?"

Jodie: "I am calling to ask for information on how best to send in a query letter and a sample for a new family column idea. Is this the right area?"

Editor: "We are not accepting any query letters on ideas for family columns at this time."

Jodie: "If you will read my column, you will find it is different. In fact, my two years of research show that the column fills a void in the family area."

Editor: "I am busy and can't talk right now; if you want to send in a query letter and samples, you can get the mailing address from the front desk."

Jodie: "Thank you; sorry, what was your name?"

Editor: "My name is Jerry."

Jodie: "Thank you for your time, Jerry, and I will send in more information and check in with you later. Do you have a time frame of when I might be able to call back?"

Editor: "You can send in your material any time, but I have no idea of when I can look at it."

Jodie: "That's fine. Thank you for your time, Jerry."

But if you hear "We don't need anything; check back next year," send your material in anyway. I did.

How do they know if your column would be something they would be interested in if they have not even seen it? Not only that, but they have no idea of how the situation might change because of staff turnover, illness or a dozen other reasons.

If you should get a voice mailbox, use some of the same tactics:

1. Speak clearly. Do not rush.

2. Give your first and last name.

3. Tell a little about the reason for the call. Do not try to deceive anyone about the nature of your business.

4. State your contact number, and be sure it is stated slowly and distinctly.

5. Watch your tone; keep it on a professional level.

6. Smile. I used to think this was silly, but it does make a difference in how you go about the call.

7. End the message with a repeat of your name, number and, before hanging up, thank the person for his/her time.

Telephone Interview Tips:

A telephone interview is basically a prescreening session. Be prepared. The editor may be able to talk for just a few minutes. If you are not prepared, it will show.

Practice with a friend. Answer the "who done it" questions. I worked on responses as if I was writing a "whodunit" play, answering the all-time favorite requirements of any good reporter, columnist, lawyer, psychologist, radio-TV personality or private investigator: who, why, what, where, when, and how. I tried to have all of the answers ready. In my case, I did get to briefly speak to the editor over the phone and was able to tell a little about what I had in mind.

OK, here is where I let down my professional shield. I pretty much stumbled the first time I talked with an editor about my idea. I mean I came out with egg all over my face.

As most people would do, I scrutinized the conversation repeatedly, searching my brain and hitting my head when I realized what I had said. How stupid could I be, I thought.

I was not prepared for the interview or the conversation. My points fell on deaf ears because I was not equipped emotionally to deliver a solid sales pitch. The failure left me upset and with no idea of what to do next.

When I called back to thank the editor for her time, I said something along the lines of, "My presentation did not go as well as I had hoped. I know what it is I want to achieve, but I just kind of froze; please call me with concerns, questions and suggestions at your earliest convenience."
I think I called a couple of more times over the next two weeks. Finally, one day I called and the editor answered the phone. She said the newspaper was not interested in my column. I hung up the phone and cried.

Two more weeks went by and I was on to "bigger and better" plans when it all of a sudden hit me: I did not want to change my plan, I wanted to do exactly what I set out to do because I honestly had a burning desire to help parents raising kids in today's society. I had to go back in and explain the idea better. It was preposterous to think that anyone could make a decision based on such a poor presentation.

The newspaper editor allowed me another chance to present the case of my column, and I stuck to my original idea. The editor was amazed at the depth of my passion, and the rest is history.

Phone Tips:

• Most of the time, the editor will not be able to talk but will set up a time for a later date.

• There may be a few who have a couple of minutes to talk, and you need to make the most of that time.

Remember to try and call in the early part of the week - Monday or Tuesday - because editors are busier as the week progresses.

• Be sure when you call that it is a good time for you to talk as well, i.e. interruptions are unlikely.

• Be polite. Tell the editor you will be happy to call back if necessary.

• Your tone is important. If you are agitated by something, make the call later when things are running smoother.

• You will be evaluated on how you handle yourself over the phone. Always be mindful of the editor's situation as well as yours.

• Get pumped up. If you have a favorite song that makes you feel really good and inspires your emotions and brain to totally come alive, listen to it before making the call.

• Smile while you are talking.

• Get a friend or relative to practice with you on how to speak on the phone.

Regardless of who answers the phone and when, call back to the front desk, ask the receptionist for the correct spelling of the editor's first and last name, the correct department name, and address. Ask if the editor has an assistant and get the correct spelling of that person's name. Getting names spelled correctly is a must when dealing with most professionals, but especially with editors.

Get to know the assistants. Many times the assistant will go through the "slush" pile - packages and pieces of mail that are prescreened for the editor. If you know the name of the assistant, address the mail to that person.

Plan for your dreams and let your passion sail!

How to Write a Successful Query Letter

Rule Number 6:
Dazzle them!

Write a great query letter that gets the editor's attention in the first few sentences. Add samples of columns and then market the whole proposal to the editor in an out-of-the-ordinary package. There are examples of what I mean given below.

Submitting Your Column:

Be sure to follow their guidelines.

If the editor wants you to send in three or four samples of columns, do it. Send a résumé if you like, but be sure to tell the editor in the query letter why you think the column would do well.

Be sure to include a phone number where you can be reached, and send the information in a large envelope so things do not get smashed. Send in copies of originals. Write no more than 600 words for each one; share information about yourself and include anything you might have written before or had published. Make sure you send in copies and never originals unless you have other ones on hand. Never send in something that you will become upset about if you do not get it back.

When you do send in your query letter and copies of your columns, on the outside of the package, neatly print in bold letters: (Editor's name), per our conversation: Requested Materials.

Include a stamped envelope. Editors are pretty quirky about this, so do it. To be organized, send in several stamped, self-addressed envelopes. I prefer the 10-by-13-size manila envelopes that are snazzy, bright and colorful. Why? Because they do not get lost like the smaller ones; they stand out. Placing large, preprinted address labels on the envelopes makes them appear more like an important package, enhancing the professional status.

Make sure you have enough postage on the stamped return envelope, and do not use meter mail. Who knows when you will get those envelopes back, and the date could have already expired. The editor may not check that, but the people at the post office will.

Sometimes, if your postal person knows you, mail will get

delivered with postage due, but most of the time it will just sit at the post office, leaving you in limbo.

Jodie's Secret:

Marketing 101.

Make your first impression good. Write your column. Edit it. Take some time away from it, then edit it again. Let others read it and jot down their opinions. Put it away for several days and begin this process all over again. I also sent the information I got from all of the "polls" I conducted.

Many people do not send in query letters because they feel it just prolongs the final result. What people really should do is to send both a query letter and a sample column, or whatever the newspaper or syndicates guidelines say to do.

Market your entire package/proposal (your package/ proposal is basically all of the material you are sending) in a brightly colored, large envelope as described earlier. Everyone likes to get to the attractive things first.

I do not care who says this does not matter; it does. I get more than 15 packages a day. This triples in the weeks leading up to Christmas. My entire family has to help me keep an inventory of the items, products (including books) and tons of things for kids. The reason I get so much stuff is that if I plug something in my internationally syndicated column, it is worth mega free advertising bucks for these companies. They often respond by sending me samples of their product. The packages that catch my attention are the ones that stand out because of their wrapper. For example, a couple of years ago, Disney sent me a wooden crate full of toys based on the Looney Tunes gang. They made a new movie, DVD and tons of other things to try to remarket Daffy Duck, the Tasmanian Devil and some of the older characters of yesteryear.

The wooden crate was full of action figures, T-shirts, caps, games, CDs, movies, and even a new Barbie. What stood out to me? It was the "dazzle" and quality of the crate. It was unique, was an unusual size, and could be used to store items, plus it contained a lot of fun stuff. It was different and got my attention!

The same is likely to be true of the editors you deal with at a newspaper or syndicate. They get a lot of submissions, so make yours stand out. The stamped return envelopes that you send in with the rest of your material can be plain. It is important to make a good first impression and get your proposal opened.

Another example of how creative marketing might help: Oprah once asked for different things to be sent in for a show - things people had invented or were selling that they thought were unique. At the time, I belonged to a business women's group that had around 50 or so members. Someone came up with the idea of making large colored cubicles and gluing different items to the outside of the cubicles.

The cubicles ranged in size and pattern, making the

completed project quite large, probably about the same height as Oprah and almost as wide as the couch she kept on stage at that time.

It turned out to be such a rare work of creative marketing that Oprah actually showed it on stage and announced the group's name. This was quite exciting, and everyone was thrilled when she chose to show America what the business women in our division had come up with.

As you can see, first impressions are important and packaging is the first impression.

How to Write a Query Letter

Use the block format (every word is aligned on the left-hand side) as demonstrated in the sample. Have the pertinent contact information including the date on every piece of mail you send, and always keep a copy and/or the original for yourself.

When sending in a query letter, keep it brief, and tell the editor or syndicate how your column would be successful and benefit them. You should expect to wait awhile for a reply. This is why, in many instances, individuals do not send a query letter. But if they do send a query letter, they also send in column samples. This kills two birds with one stone. I sent in both so the editor could have an idea of what it was I wanted and also have a column to look at as an example of what I was talking about.

If you are wondering why you should send a query letter

and what its purpose is as opposed to just sending in an article or a column, here are some key points to ponder:

- Most editors prefer queries.

- Do not ignore the guidelines (submission guidelines usually can be found online) that say you should send in a query letter.

- Your query letter is a marketing tool that will sell your product.

- Your article/column is the product.

- Your query letter is a "sales pitch" for your article/column.

- The editor can gauge some of your writing ability from it (a query letter is a sample of your writing whether you intend it to be or not).

- It will provide the editor the information needed to see if someone else is already doing such a column and, if so, how yours is different.

- It may be the only way you will get your foot in the door.

- It is concise as opposed to what might be pages upon pages of information that an editor does not have the time to read.

- It is your choice, but I say save time, effort and tempers by being smart and sending both a letter and a column.

Do's and Don'ts of a Query Letter

• Provide a concise summary with bullets as I have done in the upcoming sample query letter.

• Do not use phrases such as "I just know you will love this idea." It is unprofessional and far too conversational for something like a query letter.

• Prove that you know what you are talking about. Include any research you have gathered.

• Make the opening sentence or sentences "attention grabbers."

• Offer to send in more details. Make the query letter long enough to give a good overview but not too long.

• Offer articles for a trial basis. If you do this, ask that the copyright symbol be published by your name. I did this on the advice of a lawyer. The newspaper's lawyer said it was not necessary. My attorney told the newspaper it was, and the paper did it.

What about electronic query letters?

Some companies are now taking e-mail queries. So what about it?

The Internet guidelines are new and make sending letters easier. Although not all approve of e-mail submissions, many have finally come around. E-mail submissions save time, energy, and even postage, so why not?

However, even if a newspaper or syndicate say they will accept query letters online, you do not know that it will not get deleted as spam or junk mail. Be safe: Follow it up with a hard copy.

Here are some things that will stand out in an e-mail:

• Subject line - go ahead and put "Query Letter." If you try to deceive the recipient, the e-mail may get deleted inadvertently.

• Make sure it is exactly the same as the hard copy you send, and include any Web site addresses.

• Do not attach files unless the guidelines tell you to do so.

• Do not think that spelling and grammar do not matter - they do.

• Do not send funny or unique backgrounds in your e-mail. It takes away from what you have to say, and you may not be able to reproduce it in the hard copy.

• Do not highlight certain phrases or words.

• Keep the font the same color; black works best.

• Keep the font size the same; usually 10 or 12 point is best.

• Do not send things that might seem unprofessional, as in a "humorous" e-mail signature or quote at the end.

• If you are using an odd or free e-mail address, try to hide or delete that which will appear at the bottom of the e-mail. For example, the ads in "free" e-mail addresses should be hidden or possibly deleted. Editors are not in the habit of reading ads and it may cause them to see you in an unprofessional light.

• Do not type entire words or phrases in all capital letters. This represents "SHOUTING."

• Make sure you have the right e-mail address. This will save plenty of time and grief.

Sample Query Letter

Your Name
22464 Your Street Name, Somewhere, CA 12345
888-555-0000. fax: 888-555-0000
Jodie@nooneishome.net

April 24, 2006

(Editor's name - This needs to be the name of the editor of the department where your column will run or the name of a contact at the syndicate.)

(Company Name)
(Address)
(City and State)
(Zip)

Dear (Editor's name, along with the appropriate title such as Mr. or Mrs.):

Thanks to the hoopla surrounding some of today's teen pop stars, preteen and teenage girls have a very limited selection of places to purchase modest clothing, and it is driving moms everywhere batty. There is little column coverage in newspapers or even online to help with this challenge. As a mom with four children, two of them preteen daughters, I have looked high and low for acceptable clothing only to find that the choices are sparse as well as terribly hard to locate.

In my research, I also found that many of the manufacturers who do offer modest clothing were in other countries. Hesitantly, I decided to purchase the clothing anyway. I was surprised to find that, when I washed the clothes, there was an unusually high amount of shrinkage in most of them. This experience led me to do research online for stores utilizing better fabrics and located in closer regions.

My mission had just been doubled. I knew I had to dig in and face this assortment of challenges head-on. After countless hours spent on research, I began to run reports (which turned into articles after their popularity grew) on these companies and their merchandise on my Web site. I was often asked to send these articles to schools, child-care facilities, stores, boutiques, and other Web sites.

These articles have been such a huge hit that I have now gone into great detail in them, focusing on the fabric and dye - and even listing possible allergic reactions to each one - used in various lines of clothing. This has led to a clear and concise checklist that provides invaluable buying guides not only for today's parents but also for stores.

Although my initial plan was to find a line of modest clothing for my daughters, I ended up finding not only the proper attire for them but also the best fabrics for wash, regular wear, play and health.

I am approaching you with an opportunity for syndicating these articles as an ongoing and very successful endeavor because:

1. There is hardly anything written on this topic from a mom's point of view.

2. It will enhance your visibility in communities as caring about today's teens.

3. I have polled many parents on this idea and they like it. I will include the results with this letter.

4. This column focuses on the challenges that today's parents face.

5. Together, we can help foster positive values and provide a healthy moral environment for our children.

6. This column fills a niche that parents of daughters have been looking for.

7. Marketing statistics show that girls in ages 10 to 12 spend more money on clothes and accessories than any other age group, and are accompanied by one or more adults on 90 percent of their purchases.

8. Of the two parents, moms are the ones who are found shopping with their kids 90 percent of the time.

9. This column will be pitched to the mom market, which is the largest among all spenders.

10. There are five girls to every one boy born in this country.

As you can see by reviewing my enclosed sample articles, they can be easily formatted into a column. The column will provide a quick self-help guide for anyone interested on the topic, and can be read either in the paper or online.

Please call or e-mail with any concerns, questions or suggestions. Thank you in advance for your time, and I hope to hear from you soon.

Sincerely,

Your Name
Enclosure

The Waiting Game - Why Aren't They Calling?

Be prepared to wait. Editors may take anywhere from six to 10 weeks to respond. Some send out a form rejection letter that offers no constructive criticism.

Bear in mind that these editors and staff members are busy people. Frankly, unless they are experiencing the same frustration in their own lives, your idea may not connect at first.

I'm often asked if I send query letters out to more than one person at a time. This is simply a must-do. The more you send out the more chances you have of getting an interview. If you are trying to get a column in your local paper and there are other, smaller papers around, try the largest one first. The larger paper is likely to pay more for your column.

If you are shooting for the syndicates, go ahead and approach them all. Be sure you keep good records on your dealings with each one. Do not forget to make your package stand out from the others by shipping everything in colorful envelopes that say, "Open me first."

Stand out in a crowd - better yet, be noticeable in a group!

Never Give Up!

Rule Number 7:
Ask for the interview.

Be persistent. Do what others are just thinking about doing, and get to the decision-makers first.

Submitting Your Column:

Keep in contact.

Call once every two weeks unless you are asked to call less often. You cannot be reluctant to call. Think of it this way: For every day that you are reluctant to make some type of contact, many people are doing what you should be doing - making that contact.

Remember the time Oprah had on her show a young man who had written to her every day for one year? When show ideas are sent to Oprah, her producers will ask you not to call or write anymore once she receives it. But the young man wrote every day for one year in an effort to get on the show. The producers noticed his persistence, and Oprah invited him on the show.

What does this tell you? Be persistent in a good, but regular, contact mode.

Jodie's Secret:

Do a mock interview using questions you are likely to be asked.

Set up a mock interview. I kept excellent records and did not let the words "no thanks" stand in the way of getting an appointment to begin a local column. I wrote down everything I said and everything they said, and, of course, dated it.

Listen for key words or concepts from the editors that you can use the next time when you talk or leave a message for them. For example, at the time I was trying to pitch my column I was using the phrase "making good parents better," which meant nothing to them. Then, after I heard an editor say she already had a parenting expert, I knew that I had to show her how a local parent educator could help generate positive interaction with the community.

People in the business world set store by titles. But I knew that "experts" with titles were not always real experts - I wanted tips on raising kids from the real experts, other parents.

But I still had to think like the editor might think and try to have answers for all questions that came up. I had referred to myself as a mom who wanted to make a difference. While this was true, I was also facilitating parenting classes and was a Parent Educator.

While my passion was evident, I was not giving myself an attention-getting title such as parent educator. Pick a title for yourself or make one up and use it. Always be sure you can stand behind the title and be able to demonstrate the skills that the title implies.

Top 15 Potential Interview Questions

When you get an interview, think of some of questions you might be asked. Have a friend ask them in the format of a mock interview. Remember, the purpose of some of the questions is to find out your ethics and organizational skills, as well as your writing style.

Your sample articles/columns and query letter will help an editor to get to know you a little, but editors will want to know more about your attitude and personality. After all, you will be working for them, and there are a lot of risks in the publishing or syndication business.

Possible questions:

1. Why do you think this column will catch on?

2. How would we present it to the newspapers?

3. What motivates you?

4. What do you consider to be your strengths and weaknesses?

5. What makes you stand out from others who have written along similar lines?

6. What are some of your most important accomplishments in life?

7. What are your goals as a writer?

8. Explain how you are an organized person.

9. What are you trying to achieve with this column?

10. What else have you had published?

11. Are you flexible in the format of your column?

12. How have your previous writings been accepted by mainstream media?

13. How do you motivate others?

14. What experience or qualifications make you unique

from other writers?

15. Do you understand about files and file attachments on the computer?

Once the interviewer gets you talking, you will open up and talk about things that make you tick.

Interviewing Tips:

1. Interviewing can be somewhat of a tricky situation - do not jump into an answer before thinking about it.

2. Do not tell the interviewer how many times the idea has been turned down before.

3. Do not emphasize how much money you would like to make.

4. Do say that you have been thinking about the idea for a long time.

5. As long as it is positive feedback, share what others have said about your idea, avoiding words such as "love" but using vivid descriptions that depict strong emotions: inspiring, motivating, enjoyment, thrilled, educational, etc.

6. Take any negative remarks and turn them into positive information to use in the next interview.

7. Listen carefully to the questions and take notes. The notes will help you prepare for the next interview.

8. Take note of any buzzwords or phrases that are frequently repeated. These, too, can help in your next interview.

9. Listen carefully to questions surrounding a specific situation. When something is important to a person, they will often repeat it. If it is important to one editor, it may also be significant to other editors.

10. Observe facial expressions. They could tell you how well the interviewer thinks you answered a question. Practice answering questions in different scenarios.

When the editor sends a letter or an e-mail or calls to set up a time to talk, be sure to ask if the editor has any specific concerns and make note of them. Put yourself in the editor's shoes - reverse roles and do a mock interview with a friend. This is really critical in successful self-promotion. You need to know an editor's concerns so you can be ready with the proper answers.

In watching the best interviewees on TV and listening to

them on radio, I have noticed that when the interviewee (you) is asked a question, replying with a question can do at least two helpful things: It puts the interviewer on the spot to tell you how they do something, and it gets you out of an uncomfortable situation if you are not sure what the right answer is. This gives you the perfect chance to hear the interviewer's opinion first. This gives you information before you give answers.

I am often asked how to best get children to stop talking back. I ask the questioners what they are doing now. After they reply, I am better equipped to respond with information that I think is best-suited to their family situation.

Many successful people, including Oprah and Dr. Phil, do this. They get information before they give information. It works.

Again, listen for buzzwords that each editor may use and add them to your next interviews, phone calls, e-mails or letters.

Learn from your mistakes!

CHAPTER EIGHT

Keep the Ball Rolling

Rule Number 8:
Follow up with a thank-you letter.

After an interview, do not forget to send in a thank-you note. It is important to write a letter of gratitude. Send one immediately after the interview or even after the editor has confirmed receiving your material.

Submitting Your Column:

Manners make a difference.

The thank-you note is an important tool that is forgotten by many. A poll conducted in 2004 showed that less than 15 percent of people write a thank-you note or letter after an interview. I prefer an impressive card, blank on the inside, so I can use my own words. I will elaborate on this later.

Does a thank-you note really serve any purpose? Does it score any points? Yes, it does. I used to work as a personnel consultant, and the clients, who were my bread and butter, said they really enjoyed my thank-you notes. I did not scribble some thoughtless junk, but instead wrote from the heart. They knew it took time and effort on my part to do this and sincerely appreciated it. They commented about how good it was to see someone with manners.

The thank-you note also provides an opportunity to reiterate a few key things that were discussed in the interview. If you have only had a phone interview, send a thank-you anyway. The point is to make contact again.

Here are some tips on following up after an interview:

1. Send a thank-you note. If you immediately e-mail a thank-you, mail a paper copy of it within two to three days after the interview. It is good etiquette and a sound business practice. You may ask why I am referring to your proposal as a "business" - writing a column or an article is a business.

2. Practice what to say. Do some research so you'll know a little about the company you've interviewed with, and try to incorporate some of what you learned in your note.

3. Thank the interviewer for his/her time. Always thank editors for their time. They read many letters, items and submissions each day, and appreciate it when respect is shown for their time.

4. Call four to six days after you write the note/letter. Once an editor looks over your material, questions will arise. Tell the editor you are readily available to meet again and discuss whatever might be necessary.

Sample Thank-You Letter

Here is a sample thank-you letter using the same format as the query letter:

Your Name
22464 Your Street Name, Somewhere, CA 12345
888-555-0000. fax: 888-555-0000
Jodie@nooneishome.net

May 15, 2006

(Editor's name - This needs to be the name of the editor of the department where your column will run or the name of a contact at the syndicate.)

(Company Name)
(Address)
(City and State) (Zip)

Dear (Editor's name, along with the appropriate title such Mr. or Ms.):

I enjoyed the opportunity of meeting and interviewing with you on May 13. As you can tell, I am quite excited about the possibility of working for (company name). I had no idea (company name) was the first to syndicate cartoonists back in 1942. That was the same year my grandfather began to draw the original Red Flyer wagon.

As I mentioned during the interview, the niche that my column fills has been confirmed again by Don Ruther's report on preteen girls and the stress of hidden aggression through peer pressure.

I have thought about this for some time now and have never given up on the idea of helping to solve this and other challenges that today's parents face. I think my experience as a mom and as a school counselor will enhance my appeal in this endeavor. I have enclosed one more article for you to review.

Thank you again for your time, and please call or e-mail me with any concerns or suggestions. I will be happy to meet with you again to discuss anything you deem necessary.

I look forward to hearing from you soon.

Sincerely,

Your Name

Enclosure

Jodie's Secret:

Follow through.

The most important factor in any type of success story that most people do not do is the follow-through. They get one "NO THANKS" and that is it. They head back into their same old ruts with their tails between their legs, kicking themselves for making fools of themselves and proving their families and friends right.
In my situation, the editors told me no one would want to

read about parents offering other parents advice. I knew differently because I had spent the last few years doing research that proved otherwise.

Take everything with a grain of salt. Listen but do not take everything to heart. My family and friends made fun of me for wanting to write a column. They said I would never get the column picked up by a newspaper. Then they said I would be wasting my time trying to get it syndicated.

It wasn't that they didn't agree with my idea - it was just that I was not a journalist, I had never worked for a newspaper and I did not have even one friend or connection in the business.

I knew the column would work but I had to prove it to them - and to the editor. I went to the mall and asked everyone I could about my idea. Remember, these were total strangers I was approaching. It's one of the best ways to get honest opinions.

They all seemed to love the column idea. I asked people at the park, in restaurants, in the bathrooms, at the pool, at the library, movie, church, on the street, and anywhere I could. You can do it. If a person does not want to talk to you, they will walk right past you. Don't be shy. Believe in your idea and let others know that you are interested in what they have to say. Let them know that their opinion counts.

Get as many opinions as possible from the public about your idea and send them to the editor. Keep copies of everything you send.

Sometimes things take awhile to sink in when you are pitching an idea to an editor or a syndicate. Editors are really busy and work under tight deadlines. You must have and exhibit a desire to succeed but without stepping on toes (at least not too badly!).

For example, the parenting "expert" whose column was in my local newspaper was a well-known know-it-all. He was totally black and white in his thinking process. Nothing was ever gray.

I kept in contact with the editor by sending in comments on the "expert's" columns and showing what advice I thought would better help parents than what he provided.

I sent in a column with a question-and-answer format and included local advice from parents who had already been through the situations in question. I gave their names, cities and states and any specific credentials they might have.

In other words, I assumed the role of columnist before I had it. I also kept asking for an interview while learning as much as possible about the editor I was trying to impress, such as asking if he had kids. That could provide a connection that would help the editor identify with the parental concerns my column focused on.

Sometimes, if you can make a connection, you can hone in on building a relationship. I kept asking for an interview week after week. (Hey, it worked for the guy on Oprah didn't it?)

I was assertive but not pushy . . . well maybe a little over the top, but I had found in my previous sales positions that the only way I could get to the top spot and stay there was to always be one step ahead of others. I did something to make the editor remember me at least once a month. Maybe by calling and commenting on an article I read or by sending a note on a letter to the editor I read. I kept in touch one way or another.

I am a card freak. I love cards and could probably write for Hallmark. I often send cards to a prospective column buyer. Sending cards is part of a good marketing plan. I looked for unusual cards, the kind that had interesting patterns or themes or that had raised objects on them with beautiful colors. They were all blank inside so I could write my own message.

The cards offered the perfect way for me to express myself not only in a personalized note but also in my taste of trying to be different. I wanted to make sure the recipient did not forget my name or my idea.

In writing, say what you mean, but keep the tone positive and slightly light to hold the most interest!

CHAPTER NINE

Use Your Passion

Rule Number 9:
Make a trial-column offer.

Offer your column for free for a 90-day trial basis or for however long - within reason - the newspaper or syndicate stipulates. Don't worry - it usually doesn't take long for them to make a decision.

Submitting Your Column:

Show a desire to succeed.

Send an e-mail or include a note in your submission that says you will gladly agree to let the editor place your column in newspapers and on the Internet on a trial basis without any pay for as long - again, within reason - as they would like. It sounds risky, but if they take you up on it, it won't be long before they start paying.

Don't think you are too important or too good to make that offer. Sometimes it makes a difference, and it is certainly not expected. But if you are really passionate about what you want to do, use your passion to convince the editor of your column's worth. Passion demonstrates a desire to succeed.

I was told by a newspaper editor that she didn't think there would be space for another column, but she asked me to call back for an appointment in three months because the section was being revamped. I was so bummed I cried (again). I knew this was a big fat "NO!"

But then I asked questions and found out that revamping a section is not unusual. Continually rethinking the way space is used helps a newspaper keep up with the competition. Editors also believe it stimulates reader interest. (I always thought it just made everyone mad. Why change a good thing?)

Jodie's Secret:

Guarantee your work.

When I didn't hear back soon from the editor, I called and called and called and kept saying that I guaranteed the column would be successful. I knew it would work because I had done all of the research from a massive database in written form and from the one place that would make or break the column - the people who would read it.

Finally, I spoke with the editor who said, "Well, we are going to sign off on it." Yikes! Since I had not been exposed to journalism, I thought that meant "kiss it off," as in don't call back! I was devastated since I had been waiting five months to hear from them. I sighed and told the editor I would try a different newspaper in a different town.

Then I heard, "No, that means we want you." I started dancing around and was shouting so loud that I heard a giggle at the other end of the phone. I offered the column for free. They offered me a very small amount and increased it after 30 days. That was 10 years ago, now going on 11.

The competition from numerous specialized publications, weekly newspapers and the Internet that daily newspapers faced back then was not as great as it is today. Can you imagine what newspapers contend with in today's fast-paced, ever-changing society? So when editors ask for a little more time or for more information on your idea, show some understanding and offer double whatever the time they are asking for.

Offering Your Column for Free

I know many of you are wondering about offering your column to a newspaper or syndicate for no charge, as in totally free. What exactly are the benefits?

The benefits can range from getting your column in print to bartering for other similar assignments or articles published online and offline.

If you are wondering how this barter or exchange of free work profits anyone, here is an example. Five or so years ago, I begin presenting a **Parent to Parent Adding Wisdom Award™** to Web sites who were offering a safe, fun, educational and family-friendly site. I was determined to squash porn and unsafe sites for kids after my own children received some horrible e-mails that contained some extremely lewd messages with links to even worse full-blown nude pictures.

In doing so, I approached some of the larger, well-known companies such as Disney and PBS. Many weeks passed before I heard back, but because of my constant persistence, they did contact me.

In fact, I worked with a few of them in exchange for a reciprocal link from my award, which was a graphic award that they could post on their site. For those of you who are Internet-savvy, you know that getting the right reciprocal link from a major company with a popular and thriving site paves the way for a multitude of opportunities from other large companies in boosting online - and offline - professional status.

When Sue Castle, executive producer for PBS, offered a reciprocal link, it was a major breakthrough for my endeavor. In return, I offered not only to plug current PBS events and TV programs on my site, but to also write for a sister site as a parenting expert - for free.

Needless to say, other folks with major sites began to take notice of my Keep the Web Safe campaign, and began to contact me. Among those were Nestlé's, InTheMix.org,

ItsMyLife.org and Disney.com.

By working with these companies free of charge, sometimes for as long as five years, the award program was becoming well known, as well were the **Parent to Parent™** site and my column.

In fact, the **Parent to Parent Adding Wisdom Award™** is the only award program to ever be honored by Disney.com, which includes a reciprocal link from its corporate Web page to mine. This was the first time in the history of that company that this had been done. That is huge! (See both of my sites for verification of this by clicking on the Disney.com logo.)

After I offered the award to a multitude of Web sites, and doing so at no charge for so long, manufacturers, individuals and publishers of books, toys, jewelry, games, etc., began to ask if I would review their products. It was overwhelming and took so much time and effort that I decided to charge a fee. How else would I ever be able to "review" these the way that they needed and deserved?

Today, the award program is a full-blown profitable business with a VP of Marketing and a Family Testing Team of 20 (including kids and parents).

When everyone was making fun of me doing so much completely gratis, it all made perfect sense in the end. It took persistence, patience and time - plus lots of "bartering" - but it certainly paid off. Not only do I have a profitable quality business with the award company, but also, my name and reputation have been gaining additional exposure over the last 10 years. That has brought me many other opportunities, including writing, speaking, radio, TV and books, plus plenty of "expert" status. Therefore, I think it is crucial to study all opportunities with a positive outlook, and sometimes do things for others without being concerned about what you will be getting out of it in return.

What I am trying to share with you is a lesson that has carried me throughout life: "Do unto others as you would have them do unto you." I think God is always in control and He will give back to you what you have given to others.

Life is not fair. Practice turning a negative into a positive and that will become a life skill in itself!

CHAPTER TEN

If No Means No, Do It Yourself

Rule Number 10:
If a syndicate rejects you, self-syndicate.

It's a brave and scary thought, but why not go for it? If you do not, you will always wonder about it for the rest of your life.

Submitting Your Column:

Make a bold leap.

If the editors just do not see the potential for your column, and you feel like you gave it everything you had, prove them wrong. Self-syndicate. It is a little tougher and it is not for everyone, but now that you have grown older and wiser, why not give it a whirl?

Jodie's Secret:

Dare to be your own boss.

Self-syndicate. After getting a column, making it successful, and getting it syndicated, you would think it would all be smooth sailing. Right? Wrong! Even though I was syndicated, after seven years of writing the column, there were things for me that were just not clicking as I thought they should have been. It's like with anything in life - when you first start out, most of the time you don't know enough to ask or even know what to ask for when it comes time for the syndicate to market your column. You are thrilled with anything the syndicate is willing to do and put your trust in its decisions.

Budgets, or should I say budget cuts, call the shots in the marketing department. Personally, I think that the syndicate editors should tell the columnist what they are doing to promote the column - when, how, where and why - and then listen to what the columnist has to say about it.

For example, let's say the syndicate decides to print a flier to hand out at the annual syndicate fair where the newspaper editors gather. These fliers are used as a marketing tool, and list some of your achievements as well as a bio.

Each syndicate has its own booth set up in a specific area for the editors to come by and check out what's going on and what is new. They pick up sample columns, books and fliers. What if they use the same flier over and over on you but your information has drastically changed? In fact, you sent in updated materials not once, not twice, but three times. You were told you would be able to approve the new flier before it was printed. You never got to see it, and that was the end of that.

I am adamant about people aspiring to showcase their wares the best that they can. Well, I was the syndicate's "ware," and the presentation could have been much better.

Maybe it was because I was in both inside and outside sales for many years, but marketing and advertising were areas I knew a little about, so why should not the syndicate pay attention to what I was saying.

I love the movie "Mr. Mom." A dad loses his job and the mom goes to work, leaving him at home with three kids. In the beginning, he fails miserably in his domestic duties, but with time, he improves.

The mom experienced similar problems. Her co-workers snubbed her and wondered what in the world a stay-at-home mom could bring to the top advertising agency after being out of the workforce for so long. It was her keen eye that brought back a large account after she evaluated how the agency was marketing it to the moms. Who would know better how to do this but a mom herself? Get my drift?

While my editors were nice and pleasant, the column wasn't growing very much and the advertising and marketing just weren't being done in the way I thought they would be done - like I thought that we had discussed.

One of the most important tools in any business, or just

in everyday life, is the follow-through. The syndicate's follow-through on my column was not good.

In conversations via e-mail, things get lost in the translation, deleted or put on the back burner, which would leave anyone trying to make a point perplexed, frustrated and perturbed for many reasons.

Once your column is offered on the wire, newspapers will sign up to carry it for a certain amount of time while others just copy it into their own paper and Web site without ever paying or signing a contract for it without you ever knowing it. For the ones who are running it in their papers, but are not paying, they will have to be approached about their intentions. Sometimes this leads to a new customer or they could decide to stop running it.

I would call or write to the person who had either sent in a question or an answer and ask them which paper they had read the column in.

I called editors at newspapers myself and asked if they were running the column. What does this tell you? Basically, this means that the syndicate tracking and billing system may not be up to snuff.

In addition to handling such matters as that - matters that should be the syndicate's responsibility, not yours - you may have to do some marketing on your own, and you will not get reimbursed for it.

Keep in mind that these are my experiences, but I have talked with many others who say the very same things.

It's nice to know you are not alone in your thinking and in your challenges.

If you dare, jump into self-syndication. If you have tried to get your column picked up by a syndicate and got the typical rejection letter, or even if you can't make heads or tails out of your contract a couple of years after you do get syndicated, consider making a bold leap and self-syndicate.

It involves so much hard work that you may not even begin to understand what all is involved, but implementing most of what I have already told you in this book is a good start. Many will tell you that self-syndication will be impossible to achieve because, as one friend in the business told me, one in every million columnists makes it! I don't know for sure if this is true, but never say "never" to me. Again, never give up!

At the time of this writing, I have been self-syndicated for going on four years. When I switched from the syndicate, every newspaper stayed with me except for two, and one of those has since signed on again. I have a pretty good rapport with each editor and most of the assistant editors, copy-desk editors and the billing department. Best of all I reap the benefits of self-syndication's three biggies: 100 percent of the money, marketing and mail.

To top it off, the editors are incredibly supportive of my making it on my own and seem to be thrilled that **Parent to Parent™** is continuing to grow. The ultimate pleasure of it all is that I did it my way, kept the parents in the column and allowed them to be the real experts as they should be when sharing tips that worked for them on parenting issues. I may not be rich in money, but I am rich in life as I strive to help coach families with our most precious cargo in the world, our children. After all, they are the future. They are our tomorrow. Though that may sound like a cliché, it sounds that way for a reason: There has never been a truer statement.

I will be happy to share with you the time-consuming, heart-wrenching, energy-depleting task of self-syndicating. Here are some pros and cons of being syndicated and self-syndicated, often referred to as the Ben Franklin system:

Pros of syndication:

- Free time. You concentrate on writing, your main love.

- The marketing and advertising may be done for you. This saves more time and energy. But some syndicates may ask you to help on some marketing.

- Getting one check each month.

- Dealing with one person, your main editor.

- Sending in your column once.

- Free distribution via the wire service.

- A free mug shot to accompany your column. Most syndicates will provide this.

- Status. Having the name recognition that goes along with being syndicated.

Cons of syndication:

- Losing money. The syndicate keeps a good chunk of the money the column produces.

- Losing control of knowing what marketing is being done and followed through on.

- Losing control of incoming mail.

- Not knowing if bio corrections or address updates have been made.

- Not knowing how or why certain newspapers pay the amount they do.

- Losing personal contact with the editors or editorial staff.

- Getting very little feedback.

- Not getting a pay raise - you don't control the amount charged for the column.

- Not being reimbursed for any marketing or advertising that you pay for on your own.

- Not being reimbursed for office supplies.

Are you motivated enough to self-syndicate?

If you have read through the book and thought everything, as in every single step, is too much work, then you had better stay where you are. There are no short cuts and there is no easy way to get syndicated. It is a lot of hard work and requires a lot of time and patience.

Here are questions to ask yourself that might provide insight into whether or not you have what it takes to self-syndicate:

• Can you call a total stranger and tell them about what you are trying to accomplish? It is called a "cold call." If you are not a fairly decent salesperson, I would forgo the whole self-syndication process unless you can muster the energy and motivation to learn how to sell. It is not self-defeating if you think you cannot. I say this because we are all a salesperson of some sort in everyday life. If you are a mom, you have to sell your idea on good behavior, homework skills and even good life skills to your kids. If you are a dad, you have to sell yourself to your kids and wife, etc. If you are an individual without kids, you are still selling yourself to your friends, family and boss. Once you begin to realize this, you can learn to make the cold calls.

• Do you have good rebuttal skills? I am not talking about being argumentative, I am talking about being assertive and creative enough to show the skeptical person you are talking to why your ideas have merit.

• Can you take rejection and turn it into something

positive? There may be plenty of rejection but the trick is to convert it into something good. Many people give up after the first or second rejection because it's a big blow to their self-respect. You may find yourself contemplating whether your column is really worthwhile. This is perfectly normal. Taking a few days off and regrouping will work wonders for these low points. Keeping a positive attitude will serve you well.

• Do you have the discipline it takes to self-syndicate? Many think they do not. But if you will study the positive side of this process, you will see that it has many advantages. There is nothing a syndicate can do that you cannot do on your own.

• Do you have good organizational skills? Even if you are not that adept in this area, you can make yourself become better organized. The main thing is to keep good records, and always get copies of agreements with dates. As for doing your own billing, should you decide to self-syndicate, it is an easy process to keep track of. It may be challenging at first, but once you get the hang of a system that works for you, things will fall into place.

Pros of self-syndication:

• Keeping 100 percent of the money. One of the most exciting aspects of being self-syndicated, is that you get to keep all the money the column produces.

• 100 percent control of the marketing. You get to make the decisions on where and how the marketing for your column is done. It is wonderful to be able to set goals, learn from experience and watch your accomplishments grow.

• Getting 100 percent of the mail. This may seem like an odd item to add to the list, but it is amazing how much mail you never see when someone else is controlling your mail. For example, people may write to you or even leave voice mail at the syndicate and you will never see or hear about it. The only way you find out that someone tried to contact you is if you have a Web site and have a system in place that allows readers to send you e-mail or a voice message. With self-syndication, everything comes directly to you.

• Getting updates made immediately. This is a great plus in being self-syndicated. If a phone number, e-mail address or any other change is needed, sending an update to the newspapers that carry your column is easy.

• Building relationships with the editors, assistant editors, copy-desk and accounts-payable department personnel. With a syndicate, you have no contact with these key people and departments. When you're self-syndicated, you have their names, e-mail contact info and phone numbers - and they have yours. This is a good line of communication and works well for everyone who is involved with your column.

• Getting feedback. Now that you have contact information on the various departments associated with your column, when you need to get feedback on anything, you can deal directly with the appropriate personnel.

• Setting your own prices. It will be up to you to set

your own pricing for each newspaper. Don't be overly concerned about the amount you ask the paper to pay. The editors will tell you what they think that they can pay.

• Setting up your own business and buying supplies at a discount. Becoming self-syndicated means that you will set up your own company. By doing so, you can reap the benefits of tax breaks and discounts at many supply companies.

• Being free to come and go when you want. You are in charge! You decide when to write a column and when to send it in. Just remember, each syndicate and/or editor will ask for a specific date for the column to be sent. Nevertheless, in the original negotiations of the contract, you set up the deadline that best suits your schedule. The same arrangements can be implemented for online publications.

• Becoming a free agent and making your own decisions about various opportunities. As your column becomes well known, many profitable opportunities will come your way. Making decisions that influence your future is now in your hands. Having the power to control your own destiny is amazing.

Cons of self-syndication:

• Sending the column more than once. You will need to send your column via e-mail to each newspaper. This may take several hours. Much of this depends on what form each editor wants to receive it in. Some ask for attachments, while others say it is OK to send it pasted in the body of an e-mail. Sending the column on the same day of the week allows each editor at each newspaper to know when to expect it. This is a crucial component in getting and staying organized. For example, there are times when, for whatever reason, my column does not get through to an editor. It could be that the newspaper's spam blocker or filter system has decided that there is something in the column that warrants it to go into spam. Often, this will happen if the column contains references to sexual or drug-related matters. If this happens, the editor will contact me and tell me the column did not arrive as scheduled. We work to find out why and to remedy the problem. This could not be done if the editor did not know which day the column is scheduled to come.

• Billing newspapers. You will need to work with each newspaper to come up with a satisfactory billing system. Generally speaking, many will ask to be billed once a month via e-mail, while a few want it both by e-mail and regular mail. You will need to bill the newspaper the same time each month. Some newspapers have gone to electronic invoicing from their Web site where you will get a user name and password. Still others will set you up for electronic payments generated right into your bank account.

• Keeping up with payments of who paid and when. Whichever way the payment comes in, you will need to pay close attention to your accounts receivable. For example, if the payment goes right into your checking account, you will usually be responsible for keeping track of that. I bill each newspaper monthly. Each newspaper is assigned a client number so I can keep track of who is paying when and for what invoice. I assign each bill with an invoice number, helping keep the process simple.

- Paying for marketing and advertising. In today's "look-at-me world," it is imperative to continue to do your own marketing and advertising to get your column in the pipeline and seen by editors. To do so, you may have to continue sending e-mails, making phone calls or sending faxes. One of the best ways to keep your name in front of them is by having your own Web site and making sure that they know about it.

How does this work without spending a ton of money? It is easy. If you can write for some of the larger Web sites, they allow you to add your bio at the end of each article. If you are associated with enough popular sites, your name and the name of your column will appear throughout the Internet. While this does take time and effort, it is the cheapest and most effective way to stay in front of potential clients.

As you can see, the Pros of being self-syndicated far outweigh the Cons.

Last, but certainly not least: Do not forget to check out the checklist at the very end of the book and get started today in accomplishing your dream!

Dare to step into the role you envision for yourself before it actually happens!

SYNDICATES

King Features
Submission Editor
King Features Syndicate
2nd Floor
888 Seventh Avenue
New York, NY 10019
http://www.kingfeatures.com
(guidelines online)

Creators Syndicate
Editorial Review Board - Text
5777 West Century Blvd., Suite 700
Los Angeles, CA 90045
http://www.creators.com
(guidelines online)

Universal Press Syndicate
Acquisitions
c/o uclick
Suite 500
4520 Main St.
Kansas City, MO 64111
http://www.amuniversal.com
(guidelines online)

Copley News Service
https://www.copleynews.com
(guidelines online w/address)

The New York Times Syndicate

609 Greenwich Street, 6th Floor
New York, NY 10014
nytsf@nytimes.com
Phone: 212-499-3300

Tribune Media Services
http://tms.tribune.com
(guidelines online w/address)

United Media
(includes United Feature Syndicate and Newspaper Enterprise Association) NEA
http://www.unitedfeatures.com/ufs/submissions.html
(guidelines online w/address)

Washington Post Writers Group
http://www.Postwritersgroup.com/submissions.htm
(guidelines online w/address)

Jodie Lynn's Syndication Checklist:
Let it Guide You Into Syndication Success!

Jodie Lynn's Updated Must-Do Checklist:

* Believe in what you have to say and in your idea.

* Know your competition.

* Make a plan and send in a query letter.

* Ask and answer questions. Put yourself in the editor's position. Role-play with a friend and ask many questions.

* Be prepared for skeptics. Hear them out and come back with power-packed success strategies.

* Follow the steps of those who have succeeded by finding a role model, but keep your own cutting-edge personality.

* Get your foot in the door by daring to be different.

* Ask for an interview and review the top 15 interview questions. Practice a phone interview with a friend.

• Be persistent.

• Show patience.

• Never give up!

• Don't forget to send a thank-you letter, note or card.

• Review the top 10 tips for overcoming common objections.

• Follow the six "whodunit" questions.

• Offer the column on a trial basis.

• Guarantee your work.

• If no means no, syndicate yourself.

• Leap into being your own boss.

About Jodie Lynn

Jodie Lynn is an internationally syndicated family/health columnist. Her newspaper column, **Parent to Parent™**, is in its 11th year.

She is the author of **Mommy-CEO™** (revised edition); the CEO/Founder of ParentToParent.com and AddingWisdomAward.com; creator of **Mom CEO™** merchandise and acronyms, including the trademark of **Mom CEO (Chief Everything Officer)™** logo. She has appeared on NBC in a three-month parenting segment, and has made other TV appearances along with numerous radio interviews. Her writings have appeared in magazines, parenting publications, school newsletters and throughout the Internet. She also has her own radio segments, Tips To Go for Parent's Today™, which is now available for Audio and Podcast.

Lynn has contributed to two other books, "The Entrepreneurial Parent," (Penguin Putnam), featured on "The Oprah Winfrey Show" in June 2002, and "Why Aren't You Your Own Boss: Leaping Over the Obstacles That Stand Between You and Your Dream," by Paul and Sarah Edwards and Peter Economy (Prima Publisher, March 2003, imprint of Random House). She is currently working on **Mom CEO (Chief Everything Officer)™ - Having, Doing, and Surviving It All!** and is the spokesperson for BabyUniverse.com and Stacey Kannenberg Unlimited, an Imprint of Cedar Valley Publishing. See www.ParentToParent.com for more information.

She and her family live in St. Louis, Mo.

Index